I am thrilled to be able to recommend these collected children's sermons. As a seminary professor who has served both as a pastor and often as an interim pastor, I have observed over the years how few churches spend appropriate time and focus on their children in worship and how few children's sermons are done well, if done at all. Debbie Mayes is a rare exception. Sunday after Sunday, Miss Debbie would take the sermon text I intended to preach and make it both accessible, understandable and memorable for the young ones. Her theological insight coupled with her energy and creativity for communicating the gospel to children make her sermons a rare gift. Often using visuals and always using stories and mental images appropriate for young children, Debbie's sermons for children are among the best I have ever witnessed. I am delighted that she is finally sharing her creativity with the wider church.

For children's ministers and pastors looking for more resources for children's sermons (something I was perpetually searching for in my own ministry), Debbie Mayes' compilation of sermons would be exceedingly helpful. I hope you will appreciate her work as much as I have. I am thrilled to see this collection published for the good of the Christian church and the glory of God.

Sincerely,
Brian C. Brewer, Ph.D.
Associate Professor of Christian Theology
brian_brewer@baylor.edu

"Debbie has a unique ability to communicate truths from God's Word so that children (and adults) can easily understand. Her special blend of humor and biblical insight present truth that engages and transforms listeners. It is an honor to count Debbie as a friend in ministry. Your ministry will benefit greatly from Debbie's messages!"

Barry Jeffries, Lead Pastor Crestwood Baptist Church, Crestwood Kentucky

Sunday Sermons
for Kids

DEBBIE OGDEN MAYES

WESTBOW
PRESS®
A DIVISION OF THOMAS NELSON
& ZONDERVAN

WestBow Press books may be ordered through booksellers or by contacting:

WestBow Press
A Division of Thomas Nelson & Zondervan
1663 Liberty Drive
Bloomington, IN 47403
www.westbowpress.com
1 (866) 928-1240

ISBN: 978-1-9736-6021-7 (sc)
ISBN: 978-1-9736-6020-0 (hc)
ISBN: 978-1-9736-6022-4 (e)

Library of Congress Control Number: 2019904637

Print information available on the last page.

WestBow Press rev. date: 05/02/2019

I dedicate this book to my beloved and adored grandchildren.
Maggie, Harper, Miller and Lucy, your Mammy loves you.

We Need to Know the Truth

Good morning, boys and girls! This morning, we're going to play a game. I'll tell you something, and you'll tell me if what I've said is the truth or a lie—if it's true or false.

Are you ready? Here we go!

1. Jesus was born in a fancy hospital in Mexico. (False.)
2. You can find God's truths in the Holy Bible. (True.)
3. In the beginning, God created the heavens and the earth. (True.)
4. Jesus died in an airplane crash, and his body was never found. (False.)
5. Jesus died on a cross. (True.)
6. Jesus was buried and never seen again. (False.)
7. You can be your own God. Just be good and you'll go to heaven. You don't need Jesus. (False.)
8. Jesus is the Way, the Truth, and the Life. (True.)

9. When we die, we go to Disney World. (False.)

10. Jesus is the holy Son of God. (True.)

Boys and girls, you did a great job. That's because you've been taught the truth. We need to know the truth. There are many teachers and preachers teaching false messages. Where do we find the truth? We find the truth in God's holy Word, the Bible. That's why we need to study our Bibles. We need to know what the Bible says. That way, we'll know when someone is teaching us things that aren't right. We must read and study our Bibles. We should memorize as much of the Bible as we can. It is very important to know the truth. God's truth.

Please answer true or false to one more statement: Jesus loves you and wants you to know the truth.

That's right! It's true!

Let's Pray

Dear heavenly Father, we want to know the truth. Help us to listen, study, and memorize your words so no one can lead us astray or trap us with their false or wrong words. In Jesus's name, we pray. Amen.

Peace, Joy, and Hope

Romans 5:1–2

Good morning, boys and girls!

Today we'll be talking about three special words. Those words are *peace, joy,* and *hope.* In God's word in Romans 5:1–2, we're told that through Jesus and because of our faith and trust in Jesus, we are at peace with God. We are no longer enemies of God. Our sin or the wrong things we do no longer keep us away from God. We are friends of God. In fact, we are children of God. Knowing this peace brings us joy and hope.

Our lives may not always be peaceful, but with Jesus, we always have peace. We may not always be happy. Sometimes we may feel sad, but we always have joy in Jesus because we know that we are at peace with God. Things may be bad, but in Jesus, there's hope—a hope that things will get better, a hope that Jesus is working everything for our good. And we have the hope of a forever life with Jesus in heaven.

How do we have *peace, joy,* and *hope?* Jesus is the answer. Jesus is our peace, our joy, and our hope. It's all about Jesus.

Let's Pray

Dear heavenly Father, Jesus is our way to you, and Jesus is our *peace, joy,* and *hope.* Thank you for Jesus. In his mighty name, we pray. Amen.

Temptation

Good morning, boys and girls!

Today, we're going to play a game of Simon says. If I say, "Simon says" to do something, you do it. If I don't say, "Simon says," you don't do it. Let's get ready to play.

Simon says, "Clap your hands."

Simon says, "Blink your eyes."

Touch your nose.

Simon says, "Stand up, and bark like a dog."

Simon says, "Stop."

Wave at your pastor.

Simon says, "Laugh out loud."

Pretend to cry.

That was a really fun game.

In the game of Simon says, you do what Simon says for you to do, but in real life, you should do what God says to do.

Did you know that Satan—the devil—will try to trick you or tempt you into doing what he wants you to do? And it's never what God says we should do.

God's Word says in Exodus 20:15, "Don't steal." If you go to the store to buy something and the cashier gives you too much change, don't be tempted to keep the extra money. That's stealing. If you take anything that doesn't belong to you, it's stealing.

God's Word in Matthew 5:44 says, "Love your enemies." If someone hurts you, don't be tempted to hurt them back. Hurting them back is wrong.

God's Word says in Exodus 20:16, "Don't lie." If you accidentally break a vase or something and your mom asks you how it got broken, don't lie to keep yourself out of trouble. Do what's right. Tell the truth.

Satan—the devil—even tried to get Jesus to do things that were wrong. When he tried that with Jesus, do you know what Jesus did?

Jesus used a powerful weapon. The weapon Jesus used was a sword. His sword and our sword is the powerful Word of God. That's the best way to fight our enemy, the devil. You swing your sword by memorizing scripture, obeying scripture, and believing in the power of God's holy Word. Your sword will be super sharp and ready to beat the devil every time he shows up. And trust me: he shows up over and over again. So pray often, know and obey God's Word, and swing that double-edged sword to the glory of our Lord and Savior, Jesus Christ.

Let's Pray

Dear Father in heaven, thank you so much for the power your words have in defeating the devil. Help us to learn, obey, and believe the Bible, the greatest book ever written. In Jesus's mighty name, amen.

The Rich Man
and Lazarus

Luke 16:19–31

Good morning, boys and girls!

This morning, we're going to talk about a story Jesus told in Luke 16. The story is about two men: a rich man and a poor man. The poor man's name was Lazarus.

The rich man wore the best clothes, ate the best food, and lived an easy life every day.

The poor beggar, named Lazarus, was crippled. We know this because God's Word tell us that he was "laid" at the rich man's gate, which means that someone put him there. Jesus tells us that Lazarus was covered with sores and the dogs came and licked his sores. Lazarus lay there while hoping to get the crumbs that fell from the rich man's table.

Did the rich man ever help Lazarus? No, he did not. The rich man was busy enjoying his wonderful life. He was eating all his wonderful food and wearing all the best clothes. The rich man didn't need anything or anyone, not even the Lord—or at least that's what he thought!

Jesus said that the beggar died and the angels carried him to heaven. The rich man also died, was buried, and found his soul in hell. Jesus tells us that from hell he looked up and saw Lazarus, the beggar, with Abraham in heaven. The rich man called to Abraham and asked him to please feel sorry for him. He asked Abraham to have Lazarus dip his finger in water and cool off the rich man's tongue. The rich man said he was miserable in the fires of hell.

Boys and girls, this doesn't mean that if you have lots of money that you will go to hell or if you're poor you get a free pass to heaven. The only way you can enter heaven is through Jesus. The rich man was too busy enjoying all his money that he didn't have time for God. He wanted to be his own God. If he loved God, he would've helped Lazarus. He would've shared his food, his home, and his money.

God blesses us with things, not as proof of his love for us but for us to help others. Lazarus had given his heart to the Lord because the Bible says, "He was carried by angels into heaven." If we're poor, it doesn't mean that God doesn't love us or doesn't want to bless us. There's nothing to be ashamed of if you're poor. I'm sure Lazarus was glad he had to beg for bread on earth and not beg for water in hell. Jesus wants us to put our faith and trust in him. Jesus wants us all in heaven with him. But he won't force it on us. It's our choice. It's our choice to either say yes or no to Jesus. It's also our choice as to what we do with our money and our time, including whether we help others.

Let's be helpful, let's be kind, and let's be good to everyone. But the most important thing to do is choose Jesus. He's the one.

Let's Pray

Dear Father in heaven, thank you for the scriptures written about the rich man and Lazarus. Thank you for your Word, the Holy Bible. It teaches us many wonderful things about heaven and how to get there. We love you, Lord. In Jesus's mighty name, we pray. Amen.

Under His Wings

Luke 13:34

Good morning, boys and girls!

Have you ever been to a farm? I love farms! My grandfather was a dairy farmer, which means that his job was to milk cows and sell the milk. Every time I visited my grandparents, I got to have fun on their farm.

Let me tell you about what kind of animals lived on my grandparents' farm. There were of course lots of cows, bulls, and baby calves. There were also horses, pigs, and chickens. When the calves grew big, they would need to be separated from their mothers so they would stop nursing. It was always so sad because the mama cows mooed for their babies, and the babies mooed for their mamas. Animals can be very good mothers, especially chickens. When their baby chicks are in danger—either from a nasty fox licking his chops, hoping to have chicken for dinner, or from a storm—the mother hen opens her wings. If the chicks want to, they can run to her and snuggle close under her wings. If the fox wants the chicks, he'll have to kill her first. The mother hen will die for her chicks.

In Luke chapter 12, verse 34, Jesus says to the people of Jerusalem, "How often I have longed to gather your children together, as a hen gathers her chicks under her wings, but you were not willing." Jesus was comparing himself to a loving mother hen who wants to protect her chicks under her wings. Now a hen doesn't have a hand to grab her chicks and make them come under her wing. She can only open her wing and invite them in.

Jesus longed for Jerusalem to gather under his wings, but they did not want to. Instead, Jesus stretched his wings (or his arms) on a cross, open and willing to embrace all of us. Jesus was willing to die for us, his little chicks. All we have to do is run to Him, snuggle up close, and rest in the shelter of his wing.

Let's Pray

Dear Father in heaven, thank you for Jesus. Thank you for the love and protection we find in Him. In Jesus's mighty name, we pray. Amen.

We're All in the
Same Boat

Luke 8:22–25

Good morning, boys and girls!

In Luke chapter 8, verses 22–25, God's Word tells us about a day that Jesus said to his disciples, "Let's go over to the other side of the lake." They all got into the boat and set out. As they sailed, Jesus went to sleep. While he was sleeping, a big storm came up, and the winds were blowing, and the waves were crashing. The disciples were very afraid. They woke Jesus up and said, "We're going to drown." Jesus got up and commanded that the wind and waters calm down. The storm was over, and all was calm. Jesus asked the disciples, "Where is your faith?" God's Word says that in fear and amazement they asked each other, "Who is this? Even the winds and the water obey him."

These disciples loved Jesus. They were Jesus followers and they claimed to have faith in Jesus as God's son. All was well, until the storm hit. When the storm came, they grew weak in their faith, but even still, they knew where to go. They knew to go to Jesus for help. They had not fully understood just how powerful Jesus is. They said, "Who is this that even the wind and waters obey Him?" They were amazed!

We are no different than these disciples. We love Jesus, we follow Jesus, and we claim to have faith in Jesus. All is well until the storm comes. Maye it's a real storm with thunder and lightning, or maybe it's the storms of life, such as divorce, sickness, loss of a job, or death of a loved one. Then our faith gets weak. But when we run to Jesus and tell him all about it, he calms our storms. When we look back, we're amazed at all Jesus can do and has done.

We must always remember that when the storms of life come, Jesus is right there in the boat with us. Just as he calmed the storm for the disciples, he'll do the same for us. Every time he does, let us always be amazed at his power and his love.

Let's Pray

Thank you Jesus, that no matter how big the storm is, that you're bigger, and all we have to do is call for help. We can trust that you'll be there to rescue us with your amazing power. In your name, we pray, amen.

A Rock Concert?

Luke 19:40

Good morning, boys and girls!

Look what I have with me this morning, a bucket of rocks! I bet you're wondering why in the world I would bring a bucket of rocks to worship. Well, I thought we might have a "rock" concert. Do you think these rocks could sing? Do you think they can talk? Do you think they could tell you stories about Jesus? You might be surprised to hear what Jesus had to say about that!

In God's Word in Luke chapter 19, Jesus is walking with his disciples to Jerusalem. When he gets near the Mount of Olives, he tells two of his disciples to go to the next village, where they will find a young donkey. He asked them to bring him the donkey. Jesus told them that if anybody asks why they are taking the donkey to just tell them, "The Lord needs it."

The disciples did what Jesus asked. They brought the young donkey to him. They put their coats on the donkey's back so that Jesus could ride him.

As Jesus rode along, crowds were lining the streets and praising Jesus and shouting, "Blessed is the King who comes in the name of the Lord. Peace in heaven and glory in the highest." The religious leaders, also called Pharisees, did not like all the attention Jesus was getting. They told Jesus to make his followers be quiet.

Jesus told them, "If the followers were quiet, the rocks would cry out."

If these rocks cried out this morning, I wonder what they would say? Maybe one would tell the story of a young shepherd boy named David who killed a giant with a stone, proving that with God anything is possible.

Or maybe the rocks might remind us about the story Jesus told about the wise man who built his house on a rock. When the storms came, the house on the rock stood firm. These rocks might have lots of stories to tell, but we won't let them. Just as Jesus's followers praised him that day, we are here to praise our King Jesus. As long as we praise Jesus, the rocks won't need to.

Let's Pray

Dear Lord, we know you would rather hear us praise you than to hear a "rock" concert. Lord Jesus, we lift your name on high. In the mighty name of Jesus, we pray, amen.

The Bible

Good morning, boys and girls!

This morning we're going to do something really fun. We're going to pretend that we're going camping. Have any of you ever been camping? If you haven't, would you love to go camping?

When you go camping, you need something to stay in. We'll need to buy a tent, and we'll need to be sure that it comes with instructions so that we'll know what to do. We'll also need to buy a map so we can figure out where we are and where we're going. We'll need a flashlight to see what path to take. We'll need batteries to charge up the flashlight. We'll be thirsty, so we'll need water. We'll need to be fed, so we'll get some bread.

You know what, going camping kind of sounds like living! As we live on this earth, our bodies are like tents. They're just temporary houses for us. We won't live in our tents forever. When we die, our tents will be put away, and we'll have wonderful new bodies in heaven. We don't need to pack all the things that you need for camping. We can find all those things right here in this book, God's holy Word, the Bible.

The Bible is our map. We can read God's Word and find out where we should go and where we're going after this life is over. God's Word tells us what to do and not to do to have a good life that pleases God. We don't need batteries to charge us up, because God has sent his Holy Spirit to keep us fired up! In Psalm 119, God's Word says that the Bible is a lamp for our feet and a light for our path. It will help us find truth.

When we get thirsty, we reach for water, but Jesus says that he is living water. When we love Jesus, he fills us with living water, and we're very satisfied. God's Word says that Jesus is the Bread of Life. When we love Jesus and feed on his Word, our souls will be filled.

The Bible is an amazing book. The B-I-B-L-E, yes, that's the book for me. I stand alone on the Word of God, the B-I-B-L-E.

Let's Pray

Dear heavenly Father, thank you for the Bible, your Holy Word to us. In Jesus's mighty name, we pray, amen.

Like A Tree

Psalm 1:1–6

Good morning, boys and girls!

This morning we're going to talk about trees. Here are a few questions for you.

1. How many of you have a treehouse?
2. How many of you have a tree swing?
3. How many of you like to climb trees?
4. How many of you like to stand in the shade of a tree on a hot and sunny day?

I just love trees. I think they're amazing. I love the way their branches look like they're reaching toward heaven, praising Jesus.

The strongest trees have deep roots in rich, well-watered soil. The strongest trees may bend when storms come, but they don't break. The strongest trees also bear good fruit and lots of it.

God's Word compares strong believers to strong, well-watered trees. Strong believers have strong roots deeply planted in God's Word. They are watered by the living water of Jesus, and God's Son, Jesus, shines down on them with his power, presence, and blessings.

Our faith grows stronger and stronger as our roots thrive on the food of God's Word. When storms come, we bend, but only at the knees as we bow in prayer. We bend, but we never break. We are blessed, happy, and we bear good fruit. We bear kind fruit, loving fruit, grateful fruit, giving fruit, sharing fruit, letting-others-go-first fruit, merciful fruit, joyful-and-happy fruit. We have a great gardener, and his name is Jesus. He tends to us. He feeds us with his Word, he pours out his living water, and his presence shines down on us. He prunes us and smiles as we bear all that good fruit.

So grow tall, little trees, in your deeply rooted faith, well-watered by Jesus, arms reaching to heaven like the beautiful branches of a tree, bending at the knee but never breaking. I know your fruit will be wonderful and plentiful and your lives a blessing and wonder to all.

Let's Pray

Father in heaven, we want to be strong believers deeply rooted in our faith and in your Word, bearing much fruit to the glory of your great name. In Jesus's mighty name, we pray, amen.

Lost and Found

Luke 15:1–10

Good morning, boys and girls!

Have any of you ever lost anything? That's a silly question, because of course, you have. We all have. What if we lost something that was very important to us? What would we do? Would we just say, "Oh well, no problem. I can always get another one"? No, we would look until we found it.

In Luke chapter 15, Jesus tells two stories about people who lost something very important to them.

The first story Jesus told was about a man who had a hundred sheep. One of his sheep wandered off away from the others and got lost. All the sheep were important to the man, so he went to look for the one lost sheep. When he found it, he was so happy that he called all of his friends and neighbors together and celebrated that his lost sheep had been found.

The second story Jesus told was about a woman who had ten silver coins. The coins were worth a lot to her. One day she was counting her coins—one, two, three four, five, six, seven, eight, and then nine. She realized one of her coins was lost. Do you know what she did? She lit a lamp and swept the whole house until she found the lost coin. When she found it, she called all of her friends and neighbors together and celebrated because she had found the lost coin.

Jesus told these stories to explain God's love for us. God wants us to be found. He wants us to be saved. He loves us. He will look for us and call to us. He will not stop until we are found. God will not force salvation on us. He wants us to come to Him on our own, with all our hearts, ready to accept Jesus as our Lord and Savior.

Jesus says that heaven celebrates anytime one of us is saved. The scriptures say, "In the presence of angels, there is lots of rejoicing."

Once, I was lost, and now I'm found. The moment I was saved, the angels in heaven were celebrating. The moment you're saved, they will be celebrating again.

Aren't you glad that God loves us so much he never gives up on us? Me too!

Let's Pray

Father, in the name of Jesus, thank you that you love every one of us and that we're all important to you. I pray that you will help the lost here today be found. In the name of Jesus, amen.

Look to the Cross

Good morning, boys and girls!

The message today is about how much Jesus loves us. It's wonderful to read in God's Word all about Jesus. It's wonderful to know all the things he did while on this earth—how he fed thousands of people, supernaturally with just a few fish and loaves of bread; how he made the blind see and the crippled to walk; how he healed people from diseases and brought people who had died, back to life. He did many miracles. He can do miracles because he's God's Son and he's miraculous.

Today, we look to Jesus to give us the things we need. We want Jesus to heal us, to protect us and to provide for us. Sometimes we look at things going on or not going on around us, and we wonder, "Does Jesus love me?" Because if he really loved me, this would happen, or this wouldn't happen. We cannot look at what's going on around us to know that Jesus loves us. Don't do it!

When you begin to wonder about Jesus's love for you, if you need proof that Jesus loves you, all you need to do is look to the cross. The cross says it all. That's where Jesus told the world how much he loves us.

We see crosses everywhere. People wear them as jewelry; we even hang them on our walls as decoration. Every time you see a cross, you should be remembering, oh yes, Jesus loves me! Jesus really loves me. He died for me, and he came back to life, and he's watching over me and loving me. No matter how things look, seem, or feel, the cross says it all. Look to the cross! Look to the cross! Look to the cross!

Let's Pray

Dear Father in heaven, thank you for sending us a savior. Thank you, Jesus, for loving us enough to suffer the cross for us. We love you, Jesus! Amen.

Knock, Knock

Good morning, boys and girls!

Want to play some knock, knock jokes? Let's do it. Here goes.

Knock, knock. Who's there? Boo. Boo who? Oh, stop your crying

Knock, knock. Who's there? Wooden shoe. Wooden shoe who? Wooden shoe like to hear another knock, knock joke?

Knock, knock. Who's there? Orange. Orange who? Orange you glad this is the last knock, knock joke?

That was fun!

Speaking of knocking, I want to share with you scripture that Jesus taught his disciples. In Luke 11:9–10, Jesus says, "So I say to you, Ask and it will be given to you; seek and you will find; knock and the door will be opened to you. For everyone who asks receives; the one who seeks finds; and to the one who knocks, the door will be opened."

Jesus was teaching the disciples that we must ask and keep asking until we get our answers from the Lord. Jesus is not saying that if you pester God about something, that he will finally be so annoyed that he'll just say yes. Not at all! Sometimes the Lord answers very quickly; sometimes the answers come much later. But he always answers. There is no such thing as an unanswered prayer.

Sometimes the Lord says no, sometimes wait, and sometimes yes. I've heard people say, "Be careful what you pray for." Boys and girls, we can pray to the Lord about anything. We can ask the Lord for anything. He will always answer in a way that is best for us. We can trust God even when he says no. You can trust God and his answers to our prayers. He wants what's best for us. He knows better than anybody how to give us good gifts—even better than your parents and even better than your grandparents. And we know they love to give good gifts.

Jesus teaches us that when we ask of God, we receive, when we seek God, we find Him, and when we knock, God opens the door.

Knock, knock. Who's there? God is there, and he answers prayer.

Let's Pray

Our Father in heaven, thank you that when we pray, we can trust you for the right answer, even if it's no. You know best! We love you! In Jesus's name, we pray. Amen.

Change

Malachi 3:6

Hebrews 13:8

Good morning, boys and girls!

Everything is always changing. Even all of you are changing. You're losing baby teeth and getting your permanent teeth. You're getting taller. And smarter. Life is always changing. People change their clothes, their minds, their hairstyles, their hair color, and sometimes people change houses or jobs. Change is all around us. We have new people who come into our lives through the birth of a baby or a new neighbor that moves in. People die and become beautiful memories in our lives, and other times, people leave our lives because they've made changes in their own lives. Maybe they've taken other jobs, found new church homes, or moved to other cities.

Change is everywhere!

Sometimes change feels really good and makes us very happy. Sometimes change is scary and makes us upset or sad. But you know what? God knows all about the changes that go on, and you can always talk to him and tell him how you feel about it. Ask Him to help you be okay with the change and trust Him to take care of you through whatever change is bothering you.

I have good news, though. There is someone who never changes. In God's word in Malachi chapter 3, verse 6, this is what our Father God says, "I, the Lord, do not change." In Hebrews chapter 13, verse 8, God's Word says, "Jesus Christ is the same yesterday, today, and forever.

No matter what changes we face, good or bad, you can count on the Lord to keep his promises, to never leave you and to always love you. He will never change. He is the same yesterday, today, and forever.

Now that's good news for a change!

Let's Pray

Dear Father in heaven, thank you that you do not change. No matter what changes in or around our lives, that you are right there to see us through. We love you! In Jesus's name, amen.

Even When It's Hard

Acts 7:54–56

Good morning, boys and girls!

Have any of you ever watched the Olympics on television? If you have, you've watched some of the best athletes in the world. These are people who are not quitters. No matter how hard things get, they keep going, and they stand strong.

In Acts chapter 7, God's Word tells us about a man named Stephen. Stephen was being questioned by the high officials. Stephen spoke boldly about Jesus. His message was loud and clear. Stephen spoke the truth about Jesus, and the officials didn't like it. There wasn't anything wrong with the words Stephen was speaking. There was something wrong with the ears that were listening. Stephen was like an Olympic athlete. He just kept running the race. Even when his life was in danger, he never stopped taking a stand for Jesus. Let's read in Acts chapter 7 what happened when the officials heard the words Stephen said:

Read aloud Acts chapter 7, verses 54 through 56.

Before Stephen lost his life because of his stand for Jesus, he looked up to heaven and saw Jesus standing at the right hand of God. We read in God's Word about Jesus sitting at the right hand of God, or that Jesus sat down at the right hand of God, but here Jesus is standing. You know what this makes me think of? When I was a kid, if my mama was sitting in her chair, doing whatever she was doing, and if I kept acting up, she'd say, "Don't make me get up." Boys and girls, Jesus got up! The Bible doesn't say, but I believe he got up to welcome Stephen to heaven and to stand for Stephen because Stephen had stood for Him, and I believe he stood in holy restraint, allowing God's will be done—God's loving and merciful will.

Jesus can stand for a lot of things. We better make sure he's standing in delight as he watches us run the race of life. Stephen didn't win a gold medal like the Olympians; he won an everlasting life in heaven with Jesus! That's worth more than all the gold in the world.

Let's Pray

Dear Father in heaven, we want to run with our eyes on Jesus. Help us as we go for the gold. Gold being an everlasting life in your presence, and in the arms of Jesus. In his name, we pray, amen.

Beautiful Feet

Romans 10:15

(I presented this message in bare feet.)

Good morning, boys and girls!

I want to ask you something. Have you ever thought about how great your feet are? Do you ever stop and take a long look at your feet and say, "Thank you, Lord, for these great feet." Just think about all the places your feet take you and all the things your feet help you do.

Your feet walked you right into worship this morning. Your feet help you run, skip, jump, swim, dance, ride bicycles, kick balls, and climb stairs.

In God's Word in Romans chapter 10, it says, "How beautiful are the feet of those who bring good news." Good news! The good news I'm talking about is that Jesus is the Son of God. He came to earth, died on a cross for our sins, rose again, went to heaven, and is preparing a place for us. Through our faith in Jesus, our sins are forgiven, and we have the hope of a forever life with the Father in heaven.

When we think of feet going out to tell the good news, we often think of missionaries. Missionaries travel and tell those who have not heard the good news of Jesus Christ. But you know what? Even your little feet can go out into your neighborhood or into your school to bring the good news of Jesus. You don't have to have big feet to spread the good news. Just two feet, two beautiful feet and a willing heart.

Let's Pray

Dear heavenly Father, thank you for our feet and all the places they take us and all the things they help us do. Help us to remember that we are to tell others about you wherever we go. In Jesus's mighty name, we pray. Amen.

The Best of Friends

Mark 2:1–12

Good morning, boys and girls!

This morning we'll be talking about being a good friend.

(You could insert here a story to tell the children about a childhood friend of yours or a longtime friendship.)

Our Bible story this morning is from the book of Mark. It's about a group of men who were very good friends. One of the men was paralyzed. That means that he couldn't walk. His friends put him on a mat and carried him to a house where Jesus was teaching. These friends believed Jesus to be the Son of God, and they wanted to bring their friend to Jesus, because they knew Jesus could help him.

When they got there, the house was packed with people. It was even crowded outside. So crowded that they couldn't get through the door.

These friends were determined to bring their friend to Jesus. The houses back then were made of stone with flat roofs made of mud and straw. They climbed a set of outside stairs and dug through the roof. They lowered their friend into the house where Jesus was.

God's Word says that when Jesus "saw their faith," he forgave the paralyzed man's sins. Then Jesus healed his body. The paralyzed man was able to walk right out of there. Everyone was amazed! Jesus forgave the sick man's sins. Then he healed his body. Jesus is way more interested in saving you than healing you. First things first!

I love the part that says, "Jesus saw their faith." Sometimes it's not enough to just tell people about Jesus. It's not just what you say. It's what you do that matters most.

These were great friends, with great faith. They had strong muscles to be able to carry their friend on the mat and up the steps and then to lower him through the roof. Their muscles were strong, but their real strength was in their hearts—full of love for their friend and hearts full of faith in Jesus Christ!

Jesus is an amazing God! Jesus can do amazing things! Our one and only super hero!

Let's Pray

Dear Father in heaven, help us to bring our friends to Jesus, not only by what we say, but what we do. In Jesus's mighty name, we pray. Amen.

This Little Light of Mine

Luke 8:16

Good morning, boys and girls!

At the end of the message today, we're going to sing a song together. I learned this song when I was really young, and hopefully, you've learned it too. It's called "This Little Light of Mine." It starts out saying "This little light of mine, I'm gonna let it shine." You might be wondering, what light? Am I supposed to walk around with a flashlight all the time? Of course not! The light we're talking about is the truth and love of Jesus that shines through us.

The next verse says, "Hide it under a bushel? No! I'm gonna let it shine." A bushel could mean anything that keeps your light from shining. It could be that we're not obeying God, not letting others go first, not sharing, or being mean to others. We want our lights to shine brightly for Jesus, so others can see the blessings and joy we have in Christ, making them want to know Jesus the way we do.

The next verse says, "I won't let Satan blow it out." We all know that Satan is the devil. When bad things or hard things happen, the devil tries to make us sad or mad. He's hoping we won't shine for Jesus at all.

The next verse says, "Let it shine till Jesus comes." We will never give up! With Jesus's help, we'll shine for Jesus until he comes back to get us! Luke chapter 8, verse 16, says, "No one lights a lamp and hides it in a jar or puts it under a bed. Instead, he puts it on a stand so that those who come in can see the light."

That's what we're going to do right now. We're going to let our lights shine for Jesus so that all those who are here can see the light! We want the whole world to see the light and be saved!

(Lead the children in singing "This Little Light of Mine.")

Let's Pray

Dear Jesus, I hope you loved seeing us shine so brightly for you this morning. We love you, Jesus! Forever, we will "let it shine, let it shine, let it shine." In your holy name, we pray. Amen.

The Kingdom of God

Luke 17:20 and 21

Good morning, boys and girls!

Have you ever been lost while traveling with your parents? If you have, you probably remember questions like "Where is it? Or "Shouldn't we stop and ask someone where it is?"

In Luke chapter 17, we read how the religious leaders, also called Pharisees, asked Jesus, "Where is the kingdom of God?" Jesus answered by telling them that the kingdom of God isn't something that you say, "Oh see here or see there." Jesus told them that the kingdom of God is within you. The kingdom of God isn't a place we can go, see, or walk around in. The kingdom of God is within every believer in the Lord Jesus Christ.

Wherever Jesus is, that's where the kingdom of God is. When you ask Jesus to come into your heart, then the kingdom of God is within you. Everywhere you go, the kingdom of God is with you. If you go somewhere where the kingdom of God is not, you don't have to ask where the kingdom of God is. The kingdom of God will be there when you show up. That is so exciting, isn't it?

Our King is Jesus, and we are his kingdom.

Let's Pray

Dear heavenly Father, thank you for King Jesus. We are excited to know that wherever we go, the kingdom is with us. In Jesus's name, we pray. Amen.

The Sabbath

Luke 6:1–11

Good morning, boys and girls!

Today is a very special day. It's a special day because it's Sunday. One of God's Ten Commandments says, "Remember the Sabbath and keep it holy." Sunday is our day of Sabbath. It's a day where we worship and rest. We keep it holy by coming together to worship Jesus. We offer Jesus praise through songs, prayer, and Bible study. You are keeping the Sabbath holy today by being here. You're not home in your jammies watching cartoons. Someone loved you enough to see that you're here today.

In Luke chapter 6, verses 1–11, God's Word tells us how Jesus and his disciples were walking through a field of grain on the Sabbath. The disciples picked grain because they were hungry. The teachers of the law, or the Pharisees, fussed because Jesus allowed this on the Sabbath. Another time, Jesus was in the synagogue on the Sabbath, teaching. A man was there whose right hand was shriveled. Jesus healed the man's hand. The Pharisees accused Jesus of breaking the law by doing these things on the Sabbath, the day of rest. Jesus said that he was the Lord (or the ruler) of the Sabbath. He said, "Which is lawful on the Sabbath? To do good or to do evil, to save life or destroy it?" Jesus wouldn't want to make his disciples suffer hunger, or say no to a man who needed healing in his hand, just because it was on the Sabbath. Loving God and doing good to others are all perfect ways to "remember the Sabbath and to keep it holy."

I love Sunday. It's my favorite day of the week. The rest we need on Sunday is knowing that Jesus loves us. Then we spread that love by doing good to others. It's okay to rest on Sunday, but if there's someone who needs your help today, don't say, "No, it's Sunday. I'm going to rest." Say no to rest and yes to sharing the love of Jesus with others.

Let's Pray

Jesus, we worship you today. We thank you and praise you for this wonderful day known as the Sabbath. In your holy name, we pray. Amen.

A Loving Father

Luke 15:11–32

Good morning, boys and girls!

Our lesson today is about a father. The story comes from Luke chapter 15.

There was a man who had two sons. The younger son asked his father to give him all that he would receive when his father died. The father gave each son his share. Not long after, the younger son left to go to a country that was far away. While he was there, he spent all his money on sinful ways of living.

While the younger son was in the faraway country, food became very hard to get. He was really hungry. He asked for a job, and the job he got was feeding pigs. He would be so hungry that he wished he could eat the food the pigs were eating. But no one gave him anything.

The younger son started thinking about how much he wanted to go home, where his father was, home where there was plenty to eat.

He decided that he would go home and tell his father how sorry he was. He planned to tell his father that he had sinned and that he knew he wasn't even worthy to be called his son. He planned to ask his father to hire him just like his other workers. He got up and went to his father.

The Bible says that even when the son was still a long way off, the father saw him. To me, that says that the father was always hoping for his son to return. He was always watching for him. He ran to his son, put his arms around him, and kissed him because he felt so sorry for his son. He was so happy that his son had come home. The son told his father how sorry he was, and the father forgave him.

You know, boys and girls, that father had every right to be very angry and disappointed with his son. But because the son was so sorry and because the father loved him so much, he forgave him.

This story is a perfect example of how God, our heavenly Father is. There is nothing that you can do that's so bad that he won't forgive, if you're truly sorry. He will always open his loving arms to you, forgive you, and call you his child. Earthly fathers can hurt us, and some earthly father's never love their children. The love of our heavenly Father is a love that is true, faithful, forgiving, and, oh, so sweet. Love him, obey him, and if you find yourself doing bad things, stop doing them. Ask for forgiveness and run back into his arms. There you will find a love like no other.

Let's Pray

Dear heavenly Father, thank you for your great love for us. In Jesus's name. Amen.

Where's Jesus?

Daniel Chapter 3
John 1:14

Good morning, boys and girls!

(You'll need a *Where's Waldo?* book)

This morning I have with me a very fun book, and it's called *Where's Waldo?* The point of this book is to have fun, trying to find Waldo on the pages of this book. If we're going to find Waldo, we need to know some things about him. Here's a good picture of who Waldo is. When you open the book, you see so much happening on the pages of this book. There are so many people, so many different things happening, but we know that Waldo is always there. If you take the time to study and seek to find Waldo, you will find him all through this fun book. This book is all about Waldo.

I'm going to hold up another fun book. This book is God's Word, the Holy Bible. Like the book, *Where's Waldo?*, this book is *Where's Jesus?* Some people believe that the Bible is two stories. The Old Testament story and the New Testament story. There are sixty-six books in the Bible, and some people believe that it's sixty-six different stories in the Bible. The truth is that there's one story, and that story is all about Jesus. In the book of John chapter 1, verse 14, God's Word tells us, "The Word became flesh and made his dwelling among us." Jesus is the Word.

In the New Testament, we see the name Jesus. We read about his birth in Bethlehem. We read about all the miracles he did while on the earth. We read about his life, and his death on the cross. We read about how he came back to life and about how he's in heaven preparing a place for us. We may not see Jesus's name in the Old Testament, but if you study hard, seeking Jesus with your heart, you'll find him there. The Bible is one big love story—God's love for us through Jesus.

I'm sure you've heard the story from God's Word in Daniel chapter 3. It's about an evil king who was trying to make three Hebrew boys bow down to a false god. The Hebrew boys would not do it. They loved the true and living God, our God. The evil King had them thrown into a burning furnace, which is a big fire pit. The Hebrew boys were Shadrach, Meshach, and Abednego. They put their trust in God. They did not burn while walking in the fire. There's a song that goes like this:

"I saw Shadrach walking in the midst of the burning furnace, Meshach strolling as the flames were rolling, and Abednego, I see, well, that adds up to three, but there's a fourth man walking. Who is he?"

There was a fourth man walking through the fire and guess what? It wasn't Waldo. It was Jesus!

When the king saw this, he said that the fourth man looked like the Son of God.

Where's Jesus in the Old Testament? He's all throughout the pages, just like *Where's Waldo?*. You'll find him because he's there. It's all about Jesus.

Let's Pray

Dear heavenly Father, thank you for Jesus. We are so thankful for all he is and all he's done for us. Thank you, Jesus. We love you. Amen.

Oh, Be Careful, Little Eyes, What You See

Good morning, boys and girls!

Today we're going to talk about our eyes. The first thing I need to know is what color your eyes are. Raise your hand if you have brown eyes, blue eyes, green eyes, polka-dot eyes? No polka-dot eyes? Of course not. There's no such thing! That was fun, wasn't it?

God did an amazing thing when he gave us eyes. We get to see so many wonderful things. We can look into the faces of the people we love. We can see our pets, birds, flowers, butterflies, rainbows, stars, the moon, and we can read books and watch television.

Our eyes do so many amazing things. They cry when we're sad, and they twinkle when we laugh. We can blink our eyes and wink with our eyes. We can bat our eyes, we can roll our eyes, we can cross our eyes, and we can make scary faces with our eyes.

Our eyes can be very good. We can have sweet eyes, loving eyes, kind eyes, and caring eyes.

But did you know we can sin with our eyes? We don't have to, but if we're not careful, we can have mean eyes, mad eyes, stingy eyes, lying eyes, judging eyes, jealous eyes, and husbands and wives can have wandering eyes.

You're not too young to sin with your eyes. Let me tell you a little story about how easily this can happen if we're not careful.

A little boy comes into the kitchen. His mother has just made some delicious chocolate chip cookies. He asks his mother if he can have one. She says, "No, not until after supper. I don't want you to ruin your appetite." Instead of walking away, he just keeps staring at the cookies. Finally, he grabs five cookies and runs out the door.

Later, his Mom calls him in for supper. It's his favorite supper, but his stomach is so sick that he can't eat. His mom says, "What's wrong?"

He says, "I guess I caught a stomach virus. I don't' feel like eating."

His mom says, "Did you get into those cookies?"

And he says, "No."

There you go. First, the little boy disobeyed his mom when he took the five cookies, second he lied about why he was sick, and third, he lied about taking the cookies. Look how many lies and how much sin happened because he looked too long at those cookies.

There's a song I used to sing when I was a little girl, and maybe y'all know it too. It goes, "Oh, be careful, little eyes, what you see. Oh, be careful, little eyes what you see, for the Father up above is looking down with love. Oh, be careful, little eyes, what you see."

Those words are good words to learn. Don't look at things that are bad and don't look too long at things that are tempting you. Make sure that when people look into your eyes, all they see is the love of Jesus coming from your eyes to theirs.

Let's Pray

Dear heavenly Father, thank you for the gift of our eyes. Help us to look to you for help when our eyes are looking at the wrong things. We love you! In Jesus's might name, we pray. Amen.

God's Name Is Holy

Exodus 20:7

Good morning, boys and girls!

This morning we're going to talk about three little words. I hear these three words all the time. I'm sure you do too. You hear people say them, you hear them said on television, and you can read them on the internet. The three words are "oh my God." Sometimes people just say, "OMG," which are letters that stand for "oh my God."

It's funny how these words can be good, or they can be bad. It all depends on how you use them. There's nothing wrong with the word *oh*. There's nothing wrong with the word *my*, and there's certainly nothing wrong with the word *God*. Hopefully, you're talking to God or about God a lot.

If I said to you, "Oh my God, I love your shoes." Is that treating God's name like it's holy? No, of course not. If you're saying, "Oh, my God is so wonderful." Is that treating God's name in a holy way? Yes!

What's the big deal about saying "oh my God"? Well, God Himself tells us what the big deal is. In Exodus chapter 20, verse 7, God says to us, "You shall not misuse the name of the Lord your God. To *misuse* means "to use in the wrong way or a bad way." God didn't say, "I wish you'd try not to misuse My name." He said, "You shall not!" It's one of the Ten Commandments.

Jesus had something to say about it too. Remember the Lord's Prayer? "Our Father in heaven, hallowed be your name." Do you know that *hallowed* means "holy"? God and his name are holy.

I've heard people misuse Jesus's name too. We need to be careful how we use God's name and Jesus's name. They're holy, and their names are holy.

Let's Pray

Father God, please forgive us when we've misused your name. Help us to always remember to not use your name in the wrong way. In the holy name of Jesus we pray. Amen.

Planting Seeds

Mark 4:1–20

(You'll need a large seed, such as a pumpkin seed, so it can be seen well.)

Good morning, boys and girls!

Do you like to pretend? How many of you little girls like to pretend to be a princess or a mommy? What about you little boys? Do you like to pretend to be a fireman or a super hero? When I was a little girl, I loved to pretend.

Today we're going to pretend that this seed is a little boy or a little girl. We need to plant the seed so that it grows up to be a beautiful plant. Let's play a game. I'll tell you where I think we should plant it, and you tell me whether or not you think it's a good idea.

How about if I take the seed outside and throw it in the street? Do you think it will grow in the street? Of course not. Some bird might fly over and say, "Hmmmm, that looks like a good snack. I think I'll swoop down and eat it." What about if we plant it on a pile of rocks? Do you think it would grow on a pile of rocks? Of course not. There's no dirt for it to grow in, and if it rained, the seed would just wash away, or on a really hot day, the sun might burn it up. What if I just threw it in a bed of weeds? Would that work? Of course not. The weeds would strangle it, and it would never grow very big.

What if we planted it in a nice garden where there was plenty of good dirt and sunshine and the seed was able to get wet when it rained? Yes, that would be a great place to plant this seed. We could pretend that the good dirt was the study of the Bible. The rain could be prayers being prayed over you or by you, and the sunshine could be all the praise you give Jesus when you sing to or say thank you to Jesus. All this would cause you to grow closer to the Lord, and your stems reaching out would be the love of Jesus in you reaching out to your friends and family.

Jesus taught a story found in Mark chapter 4 about a farmer who planted a seed. Jesus was pretending the seed was the Word of God, just like we've been pretending that the seed was a little boy or girl.

I want to plant a "word" seed in your right now. Listen carefully. "Jesus love you." Although you can't see him, he's here, and he loves you very much. When you're sad, scared, or even mad, just let that seed grow inside you as you say, "Jesus loves me. This I know. For the Bible tells me so."

Let's Pray

Dear Jesus, thank you so much for all these children. I pray the gospel seed sown today will bring forth happy, healthy grown-ups devoted to you. Amen.

He Sent Them Out

Luke 9:1–9

Good morning, boys and girls!

This morning I brought a cookbook. In this cookbook is my favorite recipe for red velvet cake. When I follow the instructions and do what the recipe says to do, the cake turns out so good. I spread the frosting, serve it up, and share it with others.

If I only read the instructions but never follow the instructions, then there wouldn't be a cake to spread frosting on. There wouldn't be anything to serve up and share with others.

This makes me think about how Jesus gave great instructions to his disciples. After instructing them, he sent them out so they could spread the good news of Jesus. They could share what they knew about Jesus with others.

We are called by Jesus to do the same thing. If we do the things Jesus asks us to do, there will be lots of good news to spread. The truth of Jesus will be served up and shared with others.

When we obey Jesus, and spend time in prayer and in his Word, doing his will is a "piece of cake"! No matter how you slice it, doing what Jesus asks us to do is always the right thing to do.

Spread the love of Jesus, and your life will be much sweeter.

Let's Pray

Dear Jesus, please help us as we go out and spread your love and your truths with others. You are so sweet, and we love you very much. Amen.

Remember to Pray

Mark 1:35

Good morning, boys and girls!

Listen closely to what Jesus did. (Read Mark chapter 1, verse 35)

Jesus gives us a very good example as to how our prayer lives should be. Jesus got up very early in the morning, while he was rested from a good night's sleep, and before the busyness and noise of the day began. He went where he could be alone so he wouldn't have any interruptions. While others were snoring in their beds, Jesus was talking to his heavenly Father. Jesus prayed in a quiet and lonely place.

Being children, you cannot leave your house all alone while it's dark. That wouldn't be safe for children. Here's what you can do. As soon as your eyes open in the mornings say, "Good morning, Jesus." Then quickly tell him how much you love him, how wonderful he is, and thank him. You can whisper, "Jesus, I'll talk to you later in the day when I can be alone and have more time with you."

Then throughout the day as you're playing, for example, maybe you and your friends are riding your bikes, and you just take a quick moment to quietly say, "Thank you, Jesus, I'm having so much fun," or maybe Mom calls to you and your friends and says, "Anybody want a snack?" and you can quietly say to Jesus, "Thank you, Jesus. The snack is delicious."

Later in the day when you're alone in your room, you can kneel down by your bed and have a nice, long talk with Jesus. Or if you're alone in your yard, you can sit under a tree and spend some time talking with Jesus.

As the day ends, all snuggled in your bed and as you drift off to sleep, you can say, "Thank you, Jesus, for this day. I love you. Good night and, oh yes, Jesus, I'll see you in the morning."

Let's Pray

Dear Father God, thank you so much for Jesus. Thank you so much for prayer and how we can talk to you anytime anywhere about anything. In Jesus's name. Amen.

Over and Over Again

(Forgiveness)
Matthew 18:21–22

Good morning, boys and girls!

(Use a pencil today for the visual.)

Is this a toothbrush? How about a hairbrush? That's right! It's a pencil. We sharpen this end and write with it. Then when we make a mistake, we use this end to erase it. We then write some more and erase some more until the eraser is all gone. Then guess what? We have to buy a new pencil.

When we write, we make mistakes. As we live, we also make mistakes. That's why God sent Jesus to die on a cross, to erase our mistakes. When we sin, we can ask God to forgive us, and because of Jesus, God will erase our mistakes, and unlike this pencil, God's eraser never wears out.

You know what else? Just like God forgives us over and over again, Jesus teaches us that we should forgive other people over and over again.

In God's Word in the book of Matthew, Peter asked Jesus, "How many times should I forgive someone for sinning against me?" Peter said, "Should I forgive them seven times?" (I think Peter thought Jesus would be really impressed with him being willing to forgive someone seven times.)

Jesus said, "No. Seventy times seven times." That's so many times that you couldn't keep a record of it all. Jesus was saying that we should forgive them so many times that we can't keep a record. You are to forgive over and over again.

We all need God's forgiveness, and we all need to remember that Jesus wants us to forgive others over and over again. God doesn't keep score of our sins, and we're not to keep score of others sins against us.

Let's Pray

Dear Jesus, we all make mistakes. Thank you for coming to erase all those mistakes. Help us to forgive others the same way you forgive us, over and over and over and over again. Amen.

God Knows the Number of Hairs on Your Head

Luke 12:6–7

Good morning, boys and girls!

(Bring a jar full of small candy pieces or anything small that they can guess how many.)

Today we're going to play a guessing game. I have a jar full of candy pieces, and I want you to look very closely and guess how many are in here.

Any guesses? Wow, those were good guesses. Some of you got close, and some of you didn't get close at all. There are _____ pieces of candy in this jar. Wouldn't it be neat if someone could just look at the jar and say, "Oh, I know. There's _____ candy pieces in the jar." That would be so amazing.

Would you like to know something more amazing that that? Did you know that God knows how many hairs are on our heads? Have you ever tried to count the hairs on your head? If you look around, you'll see people with lots of hair and some with hardly any or no hair. It doesn't matter how much or how little hair we have, God knows exactly how many hairs are on each of our heads. You know something else? God knows exactly how many birds are in the air, and if one of them dies and falls to the ground, God knows it.

In Luke chapter 12, verses 6 and 7, God's Word says this:

> Are not five sparrows sold for two pennies? Yet not one of them is forgotten by God. Indeed the very hairs on your head are all numbered. Don't be afraid you are worth more than many sparrows.

If God cares about a little bird falling to the ground, just think how much more he cares for us. I'll tell you how much more God cares for us. He cares for us so much that he sent his only Son, Jesus, to die on the cross so that you could be saved from your sins and have a forever life with Him. I am so thankful for a heavenly Father who knows all about me and loves me anyway—messy hair and all.

Let's Pray

Dear Father in heaven. You are so amazing. Knowing how many hairs are on our heads is just one of the many things that make you such a loving and amazing Father. Thank you for loving the little birds, and most of all, thank you for loving us. Thank you for Jesus, and in his mighty name, we pray. Amen.

It's What's on the Inside That Counts

Good morning, boys and girls!

(Bring an apple for the visual.)

I brought a little something to show you this morning. It's a beautiful, shiny red apple. Do y'all like to eat apples? This one really looks like a good one. We won't be able to know if it is as good on the inside as it looks on the outside until we peel it to see what's inside.

It always makes me mad when I cut into a watermelon in the summer, and it's either too ripe or not ripe enough. Some things look so good until you take a peek at what's inside.

Did you know that people are like that too? There are people who come to worship every Sunday. They're all dressed up from head to toe. They sing all the songs. They bring their Bibles. They listen to every word the preacher says. They bring their offerings, and everything looks really good on the outside.

But on the inside, they're mean, jealous, and stingy. They don't share. They don't let others go first. They talk bad about other people at church. If they volunteer at the church, they get mad if nobody says thank you. They do things to bring attention to themselves. It's all about them.

We need to be more concerned with how we are on the inside than how we look on the outside.

Jesus looks at our hearts. If our hearts are good, good things come out of us. If our hearts are good, it's easy for us to help others, to be kind, to not say ugly words or talk bad about others, and to share.

If your heart isn't feeling very good, ask Jesus to help you do things with a good and happy heart.

Just like this shiny, red apple, we can look so good, but what's inside is what matters. Ask Jesus to help you not only look good on the outside but be good from the inside out.

Let's Pray

Dear Jesus, help us to have good, clean hearts that love you. We want hearts to serve you by loving and helping others. Amen.

Our Heart's Desire

Romans 10:1

Good morning, boys and girls!

It's so good to be here with you this morning. Our message today comes from God's Word in the book of Romans, chapter 10.

The verse begins with these words: "Brothers, my heart's desire and prayer to God for the Israelites is that they may be saved."

My heart's desire for you, boys and girls, this morning and my prayer is that you all will be saved. Let's talk about how to be saved. You can't be saved by keeping all of God's rules. There's no way we can do that. We can never be good enough. All you have to do is believe in your heart that Jesus is the Son of God and that he died on the cross and that he was raised from the dead. You must have this belief in your heart and words of confession with your mouth.

Salvation is a gift from Jesus. It's a gift that you must believe is yours with all your heart. A gift that you are so excited about receiving that you can't quit talking about it.

Once you're saved, you will be like the apostle Paul. Your heart's desire will be to see others saved. When you have something as wonderful as Jesus, you want to see others receive this wonderful gift of salvation too.

Let's Pray

Dear heavenly Father, your Word says that everyone who calls on the name of the Lord will be saved. I pray for those here today who have not believed in their hearts and confessed with their mouths that Jesus is Lord. It is our heart's desire that all would be saved in Jesus's name, amen.

Our Final Destination—Heaven

John 14:6

Good morning, boys and girls!

Do you ever think about heaven?

What are some things that you wonder about heaven?

Do you ever think about how you get there or what you need to do to get ready?

Let me help you with some of those questions and thoughts. First, let me explain how you get to heaven. Jesus said in John chapter 14, verse 6, "I am the Way, and the Truth, and the Life. No one comes to the Father except through me."

Believing that Jesus is the Son of God and that he died on the cross to pay for our sins, believing that he came back to life and is your living Savior, and by putting your trust in Him is the only ticket that you'll need to get into heaven.

You may be wondering how you make the trip. There are two ways. If you die, and you have asked Jesus to save you, then you go to heaven. Another way is if Jesus comes back to get us before we die. This is called the Second Coming. In the book of John, chapter 14, when Jesus was preparing to leave this earth and return to heaven, he told his disciples, "I am going to prepare a place for you, and if I go and prepare a place for you, I will come back and take you to be with me that you also may be where I am."

If we don't die first, Jesus will come in the clouds and take all the believers in Christ with him to heaven. You don't even need to pack a suitcase. You won't need your favorite toy, toothbrush, or even clean underwear. Jesus will have everything you need waiting for you in heaven.

God doesn't tell us all we want to know about heaven. There is some information in the Bible, but most of it is a big secret. If you think of the most beautiful place you've ever seen and the happiest you've ever been, heaven will still be way more than you could've ever imagined.

When we get to heaven and see Jesus and the angels and all our family and friends who are already there, and all the beautiful flowers, mountains, and the beautiful homes he has for us, we'll be running around saying, "All this, and all this and, Jesus, even all this?"

Don't ever be afraid. Trust Jesus. He loves you more than anybody you know. Heaven is going to be worth it all. Jesus is there—the one we sing to, the one we pray to, the one who died on a cross for you and who is alive and getting everything ready. Trust Jesus, precious children. Trust Jesus!

Let's Pray

Dear Jesus, thank you for heaven. Thank you for all you're doing right now to make it so much fun. Most of all, thank you for saving us. We don't have to do anything but believe. We love you, Jesus. Amen.

Happy New Year

Acts 13:13–52

Good morning, boys and girls!

Happy New Year! I have good news for the year _____. God is still on his throne, and Jesus still sits at his right hand. Our heavenly Father still hears us when we pray. He still loves us. He is still faithful to do what he says. Faith in Jesus still saves us from our sins. It's a new year, serving the same faithful, loving, giving, and forgiving God.

We don't know what this year holds, but we know who holds this year's future. Yes, boys and girls, God holds our future.

In Acts chapter 13, verses 13–52, Paul is preaching the good news about Jesus. He reminded his listeners of God's faithfulness in years before and how God promised to send a savior, and he did. That Savior is Jesus.

A new year full of the good news of Jesus Christ! Jesus has risen, and through your faith and trust in Him, you have the hope of a forever life with Him and all who believe in Him.

Happy New Year, boys and girls! Learn to trust and lean on Jesus.

Let's Pray

Dear Father in heaven, thank you for our savior Jesus. Thank you for your faithfulness, moment by moment, day by day, and year by year. Help us to learn to lean on you. In the great name of Jesus, we pray. Amen.

Don't Be Mean Back

Matthew 5:44

(Valentine's Day Sermon)

Good morning, boys and girls!

I love the month of February. Would you like to know why? It's because Valentine's Day is in the month of February. I love Valentine's Day! Valentine cards always have lots of hearts on them. When you see a heart, what do you think of? *Love!* That's right. Let's think of some people we love. I know you all love your parents and grandparents, sisters and brothers, aunts, uncles and cousins. It's easy to love these people, because they love us too.

But what about people who are hard to love? What about the meanies? We all know some of them, right? Maybe they hit us, push us. Perhaps they say things that are not true about us or even steal from us. When they do these things to us, are we supposed to do the same things to them? No! We certainly are not to do that. When they do wrong, we do right. When they do the wrong things, we do the right things.

Jesus tells us to love our enemies. If we only love those who love us, what is so great about that? Anybody can do that. Through Jesus, we can love our enemies.

Jesus says that when we love our enemies, we are acting like children of God. When someone does something mean, before you do something mean back, stop and count to three and say, "Jesus, help me. They're doing wrong, and I want do right. Give me the strength to not fight back." There's no telling how many people you may lead to Jesus, just by doing what's right.

Let's Pray

D ear heavenly Father, we want people to know that we belong
to you. Please help us to not pay wrong for wrong, but to pay
wrong with right. In Jesus's mighty name, we pray. Amen.

Easter

Good morning, boys and girls!

How is everyone on this wonderful Easter Sunday? All Sundays are special, but this Sunday is really special because we're celebrating Easter! This means we're celebrating Jesus!

There are so many fun ways to celebrate Easter. We dye eggs, hide eggs, and hunt eggs. You may have had your picture made with the Easter Bunny. Sometimes we buy new clothes, and sometimes we get presents, and sometimes we celebrate Easter with family by sharing a meal together. Those are all fun and wonderful ways to celebrate—as long as we remember in our hearts and minds that it's not about the eggs or the clothes or the Easter Bunny, but that it's all about Jesus. He's why we're celebrating. It's all about him.

As followers of Jesus Christ, we believe that Jesus is God's Son. We believe that he came as a baby and grew to be a man. We believe he never did anything wrong. In other words, he never sinned. He performed many supernatural miracles that only he could do because he is the Son of God. We know he came to earth to be our Savior. He was beaten and nailed to a cross. Boys and girls, this was not easy. It was hard. It hurt, and Jesus suffered. He suffered, and then he died. He died on that old rugged cross. He did that for you, and he did that for me. His death paid for all the wrongs.

After Jesus died, his body was placed in a tomb. But on the third day, the son of the Living God, Jesus Christ, our Savior, came back to life. People saw him, they walked with him, they talked with him, and some watched him be taken up into the clouds to heaven where he is right now. But because He's powerful and mighty and God's holy Son, he can be there, and he can be here all at the same time.

Remember: just because you can't see something doesn't mean it's not real. You can't see the wind, but you can feel it and know it's there. We can feel the presence of Jesus and know he's here. He's alive, and he's with us, and one day, he's coming back to get us. What a day that will be! Oh, glorious day!

Happy Easter, boys and girls! Celebrate big! Have fun and, most of all, remember Jesus!

Let's Pray

Jesus, we love you! Thank you. Please give those who don't believe enough faith to believe and call on your name for Salvation. In your mighty name, we pray. Amen.

Freedom in Christ

Acts 3:1–10

(July Fourth Message)

Good morning, boys and girls!

Soon, we'll be celebrating the Fourth of July, also known as Independence Day. Independence is a big word, isn't it? *Independence* means "to be free" or "freedom." In the United States of America, we are blessed with many freedoms. We're free to be here today to worship. We're free to decide what we're going to be when we grow up. We're free to decide where to live. We're free to do many things that effect our daily lives.

We have freedom, but you know what? Freedom is not free. Someone had to pay the price. There are people in this place today that have helped pay for our freedom. Some have served in the army, navy, marines, air force, or coast guard. Some may have fought in wars, and some may have been wounded. There are people here today who have lost loved ones while fighting for our freedom. It is great to be free!

I'm going to tell you a story today about a man who received freedom. This story comes from the Bible, which means it's a true story. There are no lies in the Bible. The Bible is God's holy Word.

One day, two of Jesus's apostles, Peter and John, were walking up to the temple. Near the gate, they saw a crippled beggar being carried to the gate of the temple. God's Word says that the man was crippled ever since he was born. He had never, ever learned to walk. His friends brought him to the gate of the temple at the same time each day, which was three o'clock in the afternoon. This was a good time for a beggar to be there because so many other people were coming there to pray. The crippled beggar lay there and begged for money.

When he saw Peter and John, he asked them for money. Peter and John looked straight at him, and Peter said, "Look at me." The beggar gave them his full attention. Peter said, "Silver or gold, I do not have," or in other words, "I have no money to give you." Then Peter said, "But what I have, I give. In the name of Jesus Christ of Nazareth, walk."

Instantly the man's feet and ankles became strong. He didn't just get up and walk. He jumped to his feet and began walking. Remember: he had never learned to walk. He was born crippled. He went into the temple. He was jumping and walking and praising God. When all the people saw him, they were amazed and filled with wonder.

The crippled man had been set free. He was free from begging, free from not being able to walk, and through his faith and trust in Jesus, he was free to be saved from his sins. You may be wondering how. It was through the name of Jesus, who paid the price. Not that Jesus's name was used as magic, but because it was used in faith. It's Jesus himself, not just his spoken name that gives our prayers their power.

The crippled man had been begging and wanted a handout. He wanted free money, or another word is *alms*. The beggar wanted alms, but he got legs! Jesus always gives us the best. He gives us what we need. The crippled man needed Jesus, and so do we. Freedom is Jesus Christ, and when you're free in Jesus, you're free indeed.

Let's Pray

Dear Father in heaven. Thank you so much that we live in the United States of America and are blessed with such freedom. But more than that, thank you for Jesus and the true freedom that comes through our faith in him. In Jesus's powerful and freeing name, we pray. Amen.

Printed in the United States
By Bookmasters